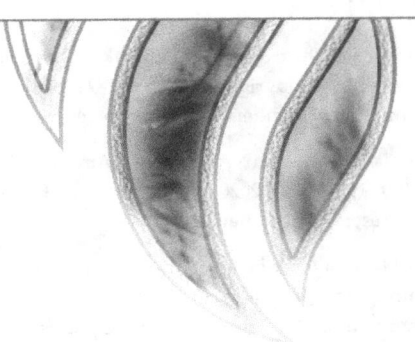

LIFE ON PURPOSE

UNLEASH YOUR *Anything but Ordinary* KINGDOM IMPACT

FORGE

CONTENTS

JESUS' MISSION

Your life-legacy is meant for high and lasting _____, but only Jesus can show you how to strategically aim at what will matter most.
(Hebrews 12:2, John 1:14, Colossians 1:15)

Jesus' Mission

Jesus stated His ultimate aim. His _____ was to *"seek and save lost people"* (Luke 19:10).

Matthew 9:36, MSG
"When [Jesus] looked out over the crowds, His heart broke.
So confused and aimless they were, like sheep with no shepherd."

Matthew 9:37-38, ESV
"Then [Jesus] *said to His disciples the harvest is plentiful, but the*
_____ *are few; therefore pray earnestly the Lord of*
the harvest to send out _____ *into his harvest."*

Note: Jesus said there are great needs everywhere, but He
identifies the one thing that is missing:

_____   _____   _____!

WHY THE WORD "LABORER"?

Jesus did not say there are too few eloquent speakers, gifted
musicians, or ___-_____ _____. He said there are too
few *"Laborers."*

Only 8% of the Body of Christ has the spiritual gift of leadership
—92% have other gifts (based off the spiritual gifts noted in
scripture being evenly distributed and test results from various
study groups).

Spiritual "up-front leaders" are responsible *"to equip the saints"*
(laborers) *"for the work of the ministry"* (Laborership), so that
every person can do their part (Ephesians 4:11-12, ESV).

"Laborer" is an _____ _____ word.

- Jesus chose _____ followers (Acts 4:13), and the message communicated all throughout the Bible is that God does extraordinary things through _____ people.

- Laborers are not seeking microphones or spotlights, but they roll up their sleeves and get things _____, engaging the mud puddles of human need.

- *"… [Laborers] no longer live for themselves, but for Him who died for them"* (2 Corinthians 5:15).

YOU ARE A LABORER IF YOU . . .

Daily seek to do what Jesus said was _____ important:

1. Love God with All Your _____ (Matthew 22:37-38)

> The greatest gift you will ever give
> this world is your _____ with God.

2. Love Your _____ (Matthew 22:39)

> Who is your "neighbor"?
> The person _____ to you in any given moment
> as you move about—every day, everywhere.

3. _____ the Kingdom Every Day, Everywhere (Mark 16:15; Acts 8:4)

Luke 10:2-3a (NASB)
"And He was saying to them, 'The harvest is plentiful, but the laborers are few; therefore plead with the Lord of the harvest to send out laborers into His harvest. Go; behold, I am sending you out . . .'"

Jesus' plan is a _____ ministry plan (Romans 10:15).

Limited by a singular, physical body—Jesus looked forward to the day when His Body (His people) would be positioned to advance His Kingdom (John 14:12).

What if *you* became the answer to Jesus' prayer request—the answer to the world's greatest need for:

_____   _____   _____ ?!

REMEMBER...

- Jesus declared Kingdom LABORERS are the missing ingredient and the world's greatest need!

- Kingdom Laborers are ORDINARY people who love God, love others, and advance God's Kingdom every day, everywhere.

1. Discuss Together: What do you think the world would be like if EVERY Christian approached daily life as God's every day, everywhere "laborer"?

2. *Every Day* and *Everywhere* describes the frequency and geography of being a Kingdom Laborer. Think about all the places you regularly go to (at least 3-5 locations). Write them down here:

You now have at least three locations in your Kingdom laborer "getting started" kit. Ask God for eyes to see the people He wants you to see in each place.

JESUS' MODEL & METHOD

God's Strategic Plan for High-Impact Living

_____ is our model to follow (John 13:15, Ephesians 5:1)!

Matthew 9:9-11

"As Jesus went on from there, He saw a man named Matthew sitting at the tax collector's booth. 'Follow Me,' He told him, and Matthew got up and followed Him. While Jesus was having dinner at Matthew's house, many tax collectors and sinners came and ate with Him and His disciples. When the Pharisees saw this, they asked His disciples, 'Why does your teacher eat with tax collectors and sinners?'"

JESUS' MODEL

1. Up-_____

Matthew 1:23
"The virgin will conceive and give birth to a son, and they will call Him Immanuel (which means 'God with us')."

You may *impress* from a distance,
but you _____ up-close!

2. Main_____

Acts 10:38
"...Jesus went about doing good..."

Jesus leveled the field where Kingdom impact
can happen. God desires to advance His Kingdom
every day, _____ we go.

. . .

3. _____ life at a time.

Matthew 18:12-14
"... If a man owns a hundred sheep, and one of them wanders away, will he not leave the ninety-nine on the hills and go to look for the one that wandered off?"

It is never _____ one.

JESUS' METHOD

1. _____ people along the way, in the mainstreams.

Matthew 9:9
"As Jesus went on from there he _____ a man..."

In Jesus' presence,
people do not feel *overlooked*, but _____.

2. _____ with people, one life at a time.

Matthew 9:9
"As Jesus went on from there, he saw a man _____
Matthew, sitting at the tax collector's booth."

When you *stop*,
you can learn a person's _____.

3. _____ _____ _____ **people, up-close.**

Mathew 9:10
"While Jesus was having dinner [spending time] *at Matthew's house..."*

Love is spelled, __ - __ - __ - __

How exciting would it be if:

EVERY Christian,
EVERY day,
EVERYWHERE,
would do what Jesus did and
SEE, STOP, and SPEND TIME WITH people
UP-CLOSE,
IN THE MAINSTREAMS,
ONE LIFE AT A TIME?

_____ are God's master plan for reaching the world
and there is NO plan B!

REMEMBER...

- Jesus declared Kingdom LABORERS are the missing ingredient and the world's greatest need!

    - Kingdom Laborers are ORDINARY people who love God, love others, and advance God's Kingdom every day, everywhere.

- Kingdom Laborers SEE, STOP, and SPEND TIME WITH people in the mainstreams of life, up-close and one life at a time.

1. Discuss Together: Take an inside look at your daily schedule and activities. With a growing understanding that you are God's master plan for reaching the world, what could you do differently this week to see, stop, and spend time with those around you?

   Need ideas? Reference the name of your restaurant server and pray for them, give your spot away in line to someone who seems to be in a hurry, buy an extra coffee for a co-worker, pack a lunch for the homeless man you see everyday, mow someone's lawn, run an errand for an elderly neighbor, write an encouraging note, etc.

2. Who are the people you regularly encounter in your every day, mainstream spaces and places? Take note of those who are overlooked, undervalued, or struggling—those who would not step inside the walls of your church and those who do not know Jesus. Write them down here, even if you do not know their name yet. Attempt to include as many people as you can think of (5-10 people minimum).

   The names you just wrote down are likely those God wants you to begin seeing, stopping, and spending time with… You now have part two of your Kingdom laborer "getting started" kit! Begin praying for those people now as a group!

JESUS' DEFINITION OF MINISTRY

As you see, stop, and spend time with people, could you:

- ☐ hold children
- ☐ sit at meal tables
- ☐ walk and talk
- ☐ spend time with a parent worried about their sick kid
- ☐ spend time with people in their homes
- ☐ engage lost people at their workplaces
- ☐ spend time on people's boats
- ☐ care for the food service needs of a large hungry group
- ☐ get up-close and care for a socially unpopular person
- ☐ Talk with a person no one else will over non-bottled spring water
- ☐ tend to sick people
- ☐ weep and pray over a city of lost people
- ☐ sit and weep with those who are grieving
- ☐ tell someone in the midst of spiritual battle that you have prayed for them
- ☐ host a dinner for a small group of promising laborers
- ☐ do the dirty, menial tasks no one else wants to do
- ☐ forgive and pray for cruel and hurtful people

All of these are things Jesus did as He *"went about doing _____"* (Acts 10:38). And Jesus continued doing good as He:

☐ cared for the needs of His mother at the foot of His cross.

☐ took time to help the man who was frightened and suffering on the cross next to His.

☐ built a morning fire and prepared a breakfast meal to love and restore a small group of exhausted guys who had been *"fishing all night,"* instead of following God's plan for them.

WHAT IS MINISTRY?

Jesus revealed His _____ definition when he said,

"The Son of Man came not to be served, but to serve," which is exactly what He was always modeling (Mark 10:45).

Jesus' ministry model simply takes a heart to care ... and to _____ _____ about it.

Ministry is meeting people at their point of _____ —physically and spiritually.

Many times, interruptions (people) *are* the ministry!

Look to God, and let His _____ tell you what to do!

GETTING OVER YOURSELF & INTO GOD'S PLAN

PERSONAL OBSTACLES

1. "_____"

   "Others are better at this type of thing and more qualified than I am."

   1 Corinthians 1:27
   "God chose the foolish things of this world to shame (confound) the wise."

   2 Corinthians 12:9-10
   "Therefore, I will boast all the more gladly about my weaknesses, so that Christ's power may rest on me... for Christ's sake I delight in weaknesses... for when I am weak, then I am strong."

Jesus called and equipped ordinary disciples who were
_____ (by popular standards of their day, and ours too!) to carry and communicate the most important message ever.

Scripture confirms, God specializes in choosing and using "_____."

2. "_____"

"I'm not good (or 'perfect') enough."

When will you be perfect?

Like John the Baptist, you can _____ to the One who is perfect, who will never disappoint (Hebrews 12:2; Romans 10:11).

3. "_____"

"I don't feel worthy."

Welcome to the "unworthy club" (Luke 17:10).

We do not do what Jesus asks of us because we are worthy, we do it because Jesus is _____!

4. "_____"

"I messed up, and have lost my value."

Peter, one of Jesus' ordinary followers, quickly confessed, "I'm a sinner." Yet Jesus said, "Come follow me." Later, after Peter fearfully denied that he knew Jesus, Jesus continued to restore Peter's purpose and value (John 21:15-21)!

You have NOT lost your _____.

5. "_____"

"I don't know enough."

Acts 4:13
"When they saw the courage of Peter and John and realized that they were unschooled, ordinary men, they were amazed, and they took note that these men had been with Jesus."

Have you been _____ Jesus? He is enough!

6. "_____"

"I get nervous, afraid, and feel paralyzed."

2 Timothy 1:7
"For God has not given us a spirit of fear and timidity, but of power, love, and self-discipline."

Discover more about prayer, fear, and overcoming in Forge's book, *Ten-Finger Prayers*, by Agnes Robertson.

7. "_____"

"I don't feel love in my heart toward them."

There are people who just are not easy to love.

You need a love-transfusion: *"God has poured out _____ love into our hearts by the Holy Spirit"* (Romans 5:5).

8. "_____"

"I just haven't done it."

John 14:15
"If you love Me, keep My commands." — Jesus

1 Corinthians 9:26-27
"So I do not run _____; I do not box as one beating the air. But I discipline my body and keep it under control, lest after preaching to others I myself should be disqualified."

Ask God to fill you with the power of the Holy Spirit to live as His Kingdom Laborer (Acts 1:8), and daily declare—

The Ten-Finger _____: *"I can do all things through Christ who strengthens me"* (Philippians 4:13)!

Remember...

- Jesus declared Kingdom LABORERS are the missing ingredient and the world's greatest need!

  - Kingdom Laborers are ORDINARY people who love God, love others, and advance God's Kingdom every day, everywhere.

- Kingdom Laborers SEE, STOP, and SPEND TIME WITH people in the mainstreams of life, up-close and one life at a time.

  - Kingdom Laborers "get over themselves" and live a TEN-FINGER PRAYER LIFESTYLE: "I can do all things through Christ who strengthens me (Philippians 4:13)."

1. Discuss Together: Which of the *Personal Obstacles* have most often (or currently) kept you sidelined from engaging as a Kingdom Laborer? What *truth* do you need to keep before you or what *action* do you need to take to be reminded how God sees you and wants to work through you?

2. Getting over ourselves never takes place until we change the direction of our attention. It is important to identify and acknowledge our shortcomings and places of needed growth. It is even more important to *raise our gaze* and allow Jesus to become the One we fix our eyes on, rather than our problems. Consider where your gaze has been and where you want it to be moving forward. Talk to Jesus about it.

YOUR UNIQUE MINISTRY

In Ephesians 2:10, we learn *"we are God's workmanship, created in Christ Jesus to do good works, which God prepared in advance for us to do."*

David the shepherd boy is a good example of this:

> 1 Samuel 17:38-40
> *"Then Saul gave David his own armor—a bronze helmet and a coat of mail. David put it on, strapped the sword over it, and took a step or two to see what it was like, for he had never worn such things before.*
>
> *'**I can't go in these,**' he protested to Saul. '**I'm** _____ _____ **to them.**' So David took them off again. He picked up five smooth stones from a stream and put them into his shepherd's bag. Then, armed only with his shepherd's staff and sling, he started across the valley to fight the Philistine."*

God has _____ created and positioned you to get involved in His plan!

You are a one-of-a-kind _____(Psalm 139:13-16)!

. . .

God wants to _____ your whole life for His Kingdom purposes:

- He can employ your talents and _____ _____.

- He can employ your _____ and interests.

- He can employ the _____ where you show up.

- He can employ your _____ _____.

- He can even employ the _____, _____ and _____ of your life.

God has designed each of His laborers with a ministry _____.

- Often it is a "_____" uniform, that allows you to naturally connect with people—in THEIR world.

- What was Jesus' camouflage uniform? How did it assist His ministry?

God's Empowerment Beyond Your Natural Gifting

There is a lot of Kingdom work to get done. And clearly there are not currently enough laborers in every facet and sphere of society.

Therefore, while God will always use who you are, what He

asks you to do may, at times, exceed your comfort, natural gifting, or preferences.

But as long as you are willing to walk by faith, He will _____ and _____ you to meet harvest needs around you, far beyond your ability!

Simply listen and _____ (Matthew 14:29-30)!

Discover historic examples of Kingdom Laborers uniquely living out their *Plan A* life. Read Forge's book: *It's My Turn: 20 Kingdom Laborers Who Changed Their World and Compel Me to Impact Mine!*

REMEMBER...

- Jesus declared Kingdom LABORERS are the missing ingredient and the world's greatest need!

- Kingdom Laborers are ORDINARY people who love God, love others, and advance God's Kingdom every day, everywhere

- Kingdom Laborers SEE, STOP, and SPEND TIME WITH people in the mainstreams of life, up-close and one life at a time.

- Kingdom Laborers "get over themselves" and live a TEN-FINGER PRAYER LIFESTYLE: "I can do all things through Christ who strengthens me (Philippians 4:13)."

- God created and desires to employ each Laborer's UNIQUENESS for Kingdom impact.

PERSONAL MINISTRY INVENTORY

Individually, do a quick inventory of the things in your life that God can employ to impact the world.

One of the greatest joys in life comes when we live out God's purpose for us. He has designed each of us like no other and His design is perfect for Kingdom impact. Perhaps that's why God seems to give us the entrepreneurial freedom to creatively apply our gifts and passions to advance His Kingdom.

What could every day impact look like if it is as distinct and unique as you are? We invite you to do an inventory of the things in your life that God can employ. It could help you discover more about how God can employ *who you are* to minister to others *where they are*.

What are your hobbies and/or recreational interests?

- ☐ Fly Fishing
- ☐ Cooking/Baking
- ☐ Running/Working Out
- ☐ Skateboarding
- ☐ Gardening or Lawn Work
- ☐ Investing
- ☐ Traveling
- ☐ Motorcycling/Bicycling
- ☐ Knitting/Sewing
- ☐ Painting
- ☐ Bowling League
- ☐ _____
- ☐ _____

What unique roles do you hold, or what season of life are you in?

- ☐ Student
- ☐ Single
- ☐ Professional
- ☐ Early Married
- ☐ Parents of Young Children
- ☐ Parents of Teenagers
- ☐ Empty Nester
- ☐ Retired
- ☐ _____
- ☐ _____

What are your tangible and financial resources?

- ☐ Guest Room or Property
- ☐ Transportation / Extra Vehicle / Ability to Drive Others
- ☐ Camping or Adventure Gear
- ☐ Reward Points / Frequent Flyer Miles
- ☐ Tools and Equipment / A Lawn Mower
- ☐ Legacy Giving
- ☐ Stock Giving
- ☐ Savings & Investments
- ☐ _____
- ☐ _____

What are some life experiences you have had?

- ☐ Travel Experiences
- ☐ Job Experiences
- ☐ Relationship Experiences
- ☐ Educational Experiences
- ☐ _____
- ☐ _____

What are some painful life experiences you have had (past or current)?

☐ Cancer Survivor
☐ Loss of a Child or Other Family Member
☐ Injury
☐ Spiritual Struggle
☐ Dark-Night of the Soul (a season of pain, struggle, or spiritual wrestling)
☐ Loneliness
☐ _____
☐ _____

Do you have any special skills?

☐ Mechanical
☐ Hospitality
☐ Art/Photography/Videography
☐ Music
☐ Carpentry
☐ Writing
☐ Caregiving
☐ Sports
☐ Education
☐ Outdoor/Survival Skills
☐ Communication
☐ Organization
☐ _____
☐ _____

Where and When Does Ministry Happen?

Think about it for a second... ministry happens in the ordinary venues of life. Not only at church, a Christian conference, retreat, or on a short-term mission trip. Here are some examples:

- ☐ With our families
- ☐ At our church
- ☐ At work
- ☐ In our neighborhoods
    - ☐ At events
    - ☐ At block parties
    - ☐ With our neighbors and their interests
- ☐ At school
    - ☐ In a dorm
    - ☐ At our lockers
    - ☐ In our classes
    - ☐ At the Student Union
- ☐ In our communities
    - ☐ In our clubs
    - ☐ In our civic organizations
    - ☐ At parent-teacher organizations
    - ☐ With our boards
    - ☐ At rescue missions
    - ☐ At ministry organizations
- ☐ Along the way
    - ☐ In the grocery store
    - ☐ At a restaurant
    - ☐ At the bank
    - ☐ At the gas station
    - ☐ At the post office

Where are the ordinary venues in your life?

_____

_____

_____

Next Steps

Now that you have begun to identify what ministry can look like (your unique hobbies, interests, passions, and more) and you know where and when ministry can take place (the ordinary venues in your life), here are some next steps to help you carry out your unique and distinct ministry:

• Look back at your inventory and see how your unique hobbies, interests, passions, and more can be specifically applied to ministry in your life situations.

• Prayerfully ask God to give you opportunities for ministry.

• Take time to search the Scriptures for verses about your giftings. Take note how others in the Scriptures used similar gift-sets to glorify God and reach others.

• Read a book about your area of unique ministry.

• Talk to a trusted Christian friend, parent, mentor, or spiritual leader about your unique, everyday ministry ideas. Brainstorm how you can use your uniqueness to glorify God and minister to others.

• Make a list of the people and places that could benefit from your ministry.

YOUR GOD-STORIES POINT TO JESUS

Mark 5:19-20

"Jesus did not let him, but said, 'Go home to your own people and tell them how much the Lord has done for you, and how He has had mercy on you.' So the man went away and began to tell in the Decapolis how much Jesus had done for him."

John 4:39

"Many of the Samaritans from that town believed in Him because of the woman's testimony..."

- They simply _____ what Jesus had done for them and entire regions were transformed.

- Has God shown up for you? More than once?

  These are YOUR _____ - _____.

Our God-Stories are an effective, simple way to _____ the lost to the Gospel message.

- A God-Story can be a moment you first believed, a moment where you went all-in and surrendered to Jesus, or simply a time when God really _____ ____ for you!

- Your God-Story (or God-Stories) should highlight the _____ that happened in your life as a result of God showing up in your life.

- Keep it short and _____. People are busy and will often tune out a long story. BUT, you can always share more later as people are interested.

- Avoid _____ and _____ words that are tough to understand.

- We can share _____, _____ with _____, and even in just a couple minutes.

- As you see, stop, and spend time with others, you will find people to share with. Making spiritual _____ or offering to _____ for them on the spot may also create helpful relational connections opening more opportunity.

Discover modern-day examples of Kingdom Laborers sharing their God-Stories and changing lives all around the globe in Forge's book, *Mudrunner,* by Charlie Marq.

WRITING OUT AND SHARING YOUR GOD-STORY

The three elements you should include in your story:

1. How would you characterize yourself before God showed up or you encountered Jesus? (For example: fear-filled, prideful, depressed, angry, etc.)

2. How did you encounter Jesus and see God show up? (For example: prayer, a sermon, a friend, etc.)

3. How did you and your life change as a result of encountering Jesus and God showing up? (For example: fear to courage, depression to joy, anger to forgiveness, anxiety to peace, pride to humility, etc.)

Write out each part of your God-Story in the three sections below.

My story _before_ encountering Jesus:

_____

_____

_____

_____

_____

_____

_____

_____

_____

_____

_____

_____

_____

_____

_____

_____

_____

How God showed up:

_____

_____

_____

_____

_____

_____

_____

_____

_____

_____

_____

_____

_____

_____

_____

How my life has changed _after_ encountering Jesus and God showing up:

_____

_____

_____

_____

_____

_____

_____

_____

_____

_____

_____

_____

_____

_____

_____

_____

_____

_____

_____

_____

_____

My God-Story: Putting it All Together

In this next space, combine the three parts to make one unified story:

MY GOD STORY

_____

_____

_____

_____

_____

_____

_____

_____

_____

_____

_____

_____

_____

_____

_____

_____

_____

_____

_____

_____

SIMPLY BRIDGING TO THE MESSAGE OF JESUS

After your God-Story, you can share the simple Gospel message in this practical way:

"This was possible in my life because Jesus died on the cross for our sins, which separated us from the one true God. Jesus then rose from the dead, so He is alive today and waiting for relationship with us. He loves us!"

End with a _____, such as:

"Is this something you are interested in?" or "Do you want Jesus to change your life too?" or "Are you interested in following Jesus too?"

Practice Sharing Your God-Story

Practice sharing your God-Story now. Make sure to include the simple message of Jesus and end with a prompting question!

Three Responses to Jesus

1. "I am _____ to follow Jesus."

Pray together with them right then! Say something like this to encourage them to begin a relationship with Jesus:

"Why don't you pray out loud with me right now and tell Jesus something like this in your own words: 'Jesus, I believe You died on the cross for my sin and rose from the dead. Today, I want to begin a relationship with You. I submit my life to follow You.'" (This concept comes from Romans 10:9).

Once someone believes in Jesus, begin going through Forge's Multiplying Movements tool with them. Start at Episode 1, so that they too can become a laborer for God's Kingdom!

2. "I _____ _____ want to follow Jesus. I am _____ interested."

If someone is not ready to follow Jesus and not interested in learning more, simply continue to love them in action, continue to share different stories of Jesus at work in your life as you get the chance, and most importantly, keep praying!

3. "I'm not ready to follow Jesus yet, but I'm _____ in learning more."

You might find someone fumbling a little bit between being ready to follow Jesus and being unsure if they are ready.

If this is the case, you can ask a simple question like "What is holding you back from following Jesus?" and then discuss whatever that is. It could be that this simple conversation removes their obstacle to following Jesus, and they decide to believe!

In other cases, they might need more time before deciding to follow Jesus. If this is the case, ask them to begin meeting with you regularly to explore what Jesus is all about by seeing what the Bible actually says about Him. Discuss any questions they may have (see episode 11 "Reaching the Lost" of "Multiplying Movements" by Forge for tips on how to meet with this person and a list of Bible stories you can use to discuss with this interested person).

- Jesus declared Kingdom LABORERS are the missing ingredient and the world's greatest need!

  - Kingdom Laborers are ORDINARY people who love God, love others, and advance God's Kingdom every day, everywhere.

- Kingdom Laborers SEE, STOP, and SPEND TIME WITH people in the mainstreams of life, up-close and one life at a time.

  - Kingdom Laborers "get over themselves" and live a TEN-FINGER PRAYER LIFESTYLE: "I can do all things through Christ who strengthens me (Philippians 4:13)."

- God created and desires to employ each laborer's UNIQUENESS for Kingdom impact.

  - Every Kingdom Laborer has GOD-STORIES THAT POINT OTHERS TO JESUS.

SPIRIT-DIRECTED LABORING

A life of high-impact involves listening for and doing what the Holy Spirit prompts.

Listening to the Holy Spirit can _____ _____ your life impact (Acts 1:8)!

_____ **for His Promptings (Acts 8:29).**

God is _____ speaking to YOU.

John 10:27
"My sheep listen to My voice; I know them, and they follow Me." – Jesus

John 16:13a

"When the Spirit of truth comes, He will guide you into all the truth. For He will not speak on His own, but He will speak whatever He hears." – Jesus

John 14:26

"But the Counselor, the Holy Spirit, whom the Father will send in My name, will teach you all things and remind you of everything I have told you." – Jesus

4 COMMON WAYS GOD SPEAKS TO US

1. **The _____.** God always communicates to us through the plain meaning of Scripture and also through Scripture penetrating our hearts based on our specific circumstances (2 Timothy 3:16; Psalm 19:10-12; Luke 24:45).

2. _____. The still small voice of God often comes through a gentle nudge inside, something going off in your spirit like a soft beeping alarm, or thoughts that are not our own but from the Holy Spirit (Mark 13:11; Acts 8:29; Acts 13:2; Acts 20:23).

3. _____. Dreams as we sleep or visions that we see while awake, almost as if they are in our imagination, can be from God (Acts 16:9-10; Acts 2:17; Acts 10:9-18).

4. _____. You may feel overwhelming compassion, heavyhearted, or compelled by God that you must do something (Acts 20:22; Jeremiah 20:9; Matthew 9:36; Luke 19:41-46).

Ask God often, "Do you have anything to speak to me?" If nothing comes to mind, simply make the wisest choices you can.

Is it Really God? — A Quick _____:

1. Does it line up with the teachings of the Bible?
2. Does it glorify God?
3. Does it advance His Kingdom (rather than my own agenda)?

If time permits, you may want to seek the counsel of others (likely for larger decisions). But in the end, _____ are responsible for what God speaks to you.

_____ is the only way to get better at hearing His voice.

_____ **His Promptings (Acts 8:30).**

This is where Laborership impact takes off!

God leads. We listen and _____. Obedience is love in action!

Matthew 7:24
"Therefore, everyone who hears these words of mine and acts on them will be like a wise man who built his house on the rock."

Take Action... When He Prompts You:

- to _____ someone.
- to slow down, stop, listen, or say something.
- to physically care for or serve someone.
- to _____ urgently for a person or need.
- to _____ a lunch or coffee with someone (ahead of time or in the spur of the moment).
- to make a phone call, text someone, or write a note.
- on what to say during your call or in your message to someone.
- to simply ___ _____ someone (silently present), place a hand on a shoulder, or lend a listening ear.
- to _____ about Jesus with someone who does not know Him.
- to uniquely advance His Kingdom.

Whenever you are with others, ask Him:

> "Do you want to speak anything through me? Do you want me to engage this person in any way?"

Be aware of the people and circumstances around you (even the small stuff) while always listening for promptings from the Holy Spirit.

What if I'm wrong?

You may not always be sure if it is Him, but learn to risk
_____ _____.

In most cases, the worst that can happen if you get it wrong is
possibly looking foolish to others. But not to God!

A greater concern—you might _____ critical impact
opportunities if you do nothing!

**When we listen and obey, God _____ lives through
us (Acts 8:38)!**

Discover how to begin an up-close, intimate life with Jesus in
Forge's book, *Is God Waiting For a Date with You?* by Dwight
Robertson.

Remember...

- Jesus declared Kingdom LABORERS are the missing ingredient and the world's greatest need!

- Kingdom Laborers are ORDINARY people who love God, love others, and advance God's Kingdom every day, everywhere.

- Kingdom Laborers SEE, STOP, and SPEND TIME WITH people in the mainstreams of life, up-close and one life at a time.

- Kingdom Laborers "get over themselves" and live a TEN-FINGER PRAYER LIFESTYLE: "I can do all things through Christ who strengthens me (Philippians 4:13)."

- God created and desires to employ each laborer's UNIQUENESS for Kingdom impact.

- Every Kingdom Laborer has GOD-STORIES THAT POINT OTHERS TO JESUS.

- THE HOLY SPIRIT EMPOWERS AND LEADS everyday laborers into opportunities for Kingdom impact.

1. Discuss Together: Up to this point in your life, how have you understood or experienced God's voice or the ways that God prompts us?

2. Individually spend some time praying:

   - In your own words tell God, "I give you all that I am," surrendering to Him, and ask Him to fully empower your life with the Holy Spirit to live as His laborer (Acts 1:8).

   - Ask the Lord for courage, committing to obeying His promptings.

   - Right now, ask God to speak to you. Pray, "Lord will You silence my flesh and the enemy in Jesus' name. I want to hear Your voice alone." Maybe you have a specific question, or maybe you just want to ask if He has anything to say to you about being a Kingdom Laborer. Listen. Write down whatever comes to mind in the space below. Confirm it aligns with the teaching of the Bible. Receive it, and as applicable, commit to obey it.

Going forward, keep your spiritual eyes and ears open
to however and whenever God may prompt you as His laborer!

JESUS' MULTIPLYING MOVEMENTS VISION

Matthew 28:19-20 (*"The Great Commission"*)
"Therefore go and make disciples of all nations, baptizing them in the name of the Father, the Son, and the Holy Spirit, teaching them to obey everything I have commanded you."

Jesus' _____ command must become our _____ concern!

With so many needs and not enough laborers, how can we possibly _____ the mission of Jesus?

Do The Math

Month	Speak to 365 per 4 months (+)	Equip 1 every 4 months (x)
4		
8		
12		
16		
20		
24		
28		
32		
36		
40		
...100		
...136		

(Taking an individual or small group through the *Multiplying Movements* tool takes 3-4 months as you Spend *More* Time With.)

1. **Spiritually** _____, **one life at a time.**

   _____ turns into many (Acts 9:26-28)!

   _____ time with _____ people
   equals _____ Kingdom investment.

2. Pass your spiritual _____.

2 Timothy 2:2
"And the things you have heard me say in the presence of many witnesses entrust to reliable people who will also be qualified to teach others."

> Your influence has to be more than passing on _____ to others.

3. _____ others, pointing to Jesus.

_____ _____: "teaching them to obey everything I have commanded you" (Matthew 28:20). – Jesus

That looks like practically equipping others to love God, love others, and advance His Kingdom daily (John 14:15; Matthew 22:37-39).

Those you train will reach people you _____ will.

> We could finish the great commission in our generation if we simply _____ more ordinary, everyday laborers!

Visit *MultiplyingMovements.com* to discover Forge resources that exist to empower YOU to multiply others, practically and powerfully!

- Jesus declared Kingdom LABORERS are the missing ingredient and the world's greatest need!

  - Kingdom Laborers are ORDINARY people who love God, love others, and advance God's Kingdom every day, everywhere.

- Kingdom Laborers SEE, STOP, and SPEND TIME WITH people in the mainstreams of life, up-close and one life at a time.

  - Kingdom Laborers "get over themselves" and live a TEN-FINGER PRAYER LIFESTYLE: "I can do all things through Christ who strengthens me (Philippians 4:13)."

- God created and desires to employ each laborer's UNIQUENESS for Kingdom impact.

  - Every Kingdom Laborer has GOD-STORIES THAT POINT OTHERS TO JESUS.

- THE HOLY SPIRIT EMPOWERS AND LEADS everyday Laborers into opportunities for Kingdom impact.

  - Laborers SPIRITUALLY INVEST in one life at a time—fueling a movement of MORE Kingdom Laborers, everywhere.

1. Discuss Together: What surprises did you encounter in the "Do the Math" section of this chapter? Consider why spiritual multiplication is both *deep* and *wide*. Is there anyone God might be asking you to *spiritually invest* in?

2. Take a few minutes to read through the list of "Tips For Multiplying" below. Then, spend some time in prayer, asking God to empower you to spiritually invest, ultimately fueling a movement of More Kingdom Laborers.

TIPS FOR MULTIPLYING

- *Be prepared.* We suggest the resource, *Multiplying Movements: A Discipleship Tool For Everyday Followers of Jesus.* Forge created this powerful tool at *MultiplyingMovements.com* to arm and equip you to practically come alongside others with organic discipleship that is easily multipliable beyond just one life.

- *Be practical.* Empower them to be able to live this life practically and without needing to be dependent on you! Share stories and examples from your life related to what they are facing. This can really help them know how to practically move forward.

- *Never underestimate the value of doing things together.* Doing fun activities or life events together provides space for deeper conversation.

- *Be second.* Point people to Jesus and Scripture. When John the Baptist's disciples began defecting to Jesus, he commented, "He must increase, but I must decrease" (John 3:30, RSV). John's example shows us how to "be second" and point toward the One who is first.

- *Make God's Word paramount.* Study God's Word with them, mutually sharing practical observations and insights.

- *Release them into God's leadership and destiny—not your agenda.* Guard against selfishly tying them to you, your ministry pursuits, or your geographical location. "Release them" over and over again. Far too many spiritual harvest fields lack laborers because the people raising them became too personally attached to "release" them into their own unique field of service.

- *Pray for them.* Bathe them in prayer. Jesus modeled this in John 17 and also when He warned Peter that rough days were ahead: "*Satan wants to sift you…but I have prayed for you*" (Luke 22:31-32).

- *Do an "inventory"—know what has helped you in the past.* List life-impacting Scriptures, books, ministries, experiences, people, audio recordings of speakers or music, annual events, etc.—anything God used to strengthen your love for Him and your love for others. Consider, how can you "pass" these blessed resources to others?

- *Introduce them to other inspiring Kingdom Laborers.* Give them a life biography in a book, video, or online message. Discuss it together. Introducing them to other "hearts on fire and lives on purpose" will encourage, inspire, and even stretch them. Go ahead, enhance their network and watch *"iron sharpen iron"* (Proverbs 27:17).

- *Encourage them in mission.* Follow up on how they are praying for and engaging the lost. Consider doing it together, to help set an example for them!

- *Prepare them for what is ahead.* Concern yourself with their roots—they will not grow taller or wider in spiritual influence unless they go deeper and broader in their spiritual depth. Ensure that they practice important spiritual disciplines: daily time with God and His Word, regular connections with other believers, prayer, Bible study, Scripture memorization, perhaps journaling, and definitely a lifestyle of worship. These practices will act as deep roots that will keep them strong, nourished, and secure when the storms of life blow against them. They need to know that storms will come. The enemy of their souls will try to bring them down. Discuss the realities of spiritual warfare and what "overcomers" have found helpful. Let them know that the more their life poses a threat to the enemy, the more he will oppose them. But remind them to "take heart" because Jesus said, "I have overcome the world" (John 16:33).

- *Address the hard issues.* God's goal for us is not to make us happy. His goal is to form us into the image of Christ. He loves us more than He loves our happiness. When God conforms us into the image of Jesus, He cuts away everything that is not like Him. In the same way, you must care so much about your young laborer that you are willing to address anything that potentially stands in the way of them becoming more like Christ. Paul addressed Timothy's tendency toward being timid and hesitant about his young age. In addressing hard issues, realize that love's most subtle enemy is not hate—it is indifference. But make sure they are convinced that you absolutely and unconditionally love and believe in them. Early in my baton-passing relationships I often say, "There is nothing you will ever do, say, or reveal that will cause me to withdraw my love for you. You are stuck with me." Unconditional love demands no retreats. Do not allow negative feedback from others (people avoiding them or being offended by them) to grow because you never cared enough to address these hard issues when you knew they existed. Otherwise, they may repeatedly strive, weep, try again, but suffer continuing challenges and unfruitfulness because no one loved them enough to help them. Love them too much to be silent. If you do not, who will?

- *Cast and release vision for their future life-impact—no matter what!* In spite of Peter's inconsistent blunderings, Jesus renamed Peter "the Rock" and gave him faith for a brighter future (Matthew 16:18). Your words could release God's destiny in someone. People wrestle more than you could ever imagine with long-rehearsed lies that the Accuser of the Brethren (Satan) has pronounced over them. Pray God will reveal truths from His Word which they and you can use to retaliate against Satan's strategy to keep God's *Plan A* Laborers immobilized. Ask God to show you *His* vision for them and what He has *"prepared in advance for* [them] *to do"* (Ephesians 2:10). Share with them what God reveals, and bless and visionize the socks off them!

Discover more tips for multiplying others in Forge's booklet *Baton Passing Relationships* by Dwight Robertson.

YOUR DECISION?

Paralyzed or Resurrected?

It's time for Jesus' Body to live out His plan!

The Kingdom of God still needs ____ kinds of laborers, doing ____ kinds of ministry (love in action), in ____ kinds of places—people who will make _____ their daily choice.

Consider the difference proven through Christian history that _____ laborer can make. Consider all the places that one difference is needed.

YOUR FIRST STEPS

**Prayerfully write out your next steps below
as you review the following:**

1. *Who* will you see, stop, and spend time with?

   Who are your first 3-5 people to begin with? Review your "every day people" (from Question 2 in the *Reflect & Respond* section, page 12).

2. *Where* will you see, stop, and spend time with people?

   Review your "every day and everywhere mainstream places" (from Question 2 in the *Reflect & Respond* section, page 5).

3. *What* pieces of your uniqueness does God want to employ to connect with these people?

   Review your "unique ministry inventory" (from the "Personal Ministry Inventory" in the *Reflect & Respond* section, pages 24-28).

4. *What* God-Story will you share?

   Review "My God-Story" (in the *Reflect & Respond* section of the "Your God-Stories Point to Jesus" chapter, pages 31-34).

5. *Who* can you take through *Multiplying Movements*, helping them develop into More Kingdom Laborers as you spend more time with them?

THE LABORER'S DECLARATION

Kingdom Laborers are God's master plan for extending His love, grace, and truth to people everywhere. We, as everyday, ordinary people are His "Plan A" and there is no "Plan B!" Join the growing movement of Kingdom Laborers worldwide by declaring these statements out loud.

Then, place these statements in a prominent location where you will frequently see them until they are displayed naturally through your life. Read and pray them often as you celebrate God's call and purpose for YOU to be His every day, everywhere laborer.

MY KINGDOM LABORER DECLARATION

1. I believe my life can become an answer to the world's greatest need, fulfilling Jesus' heart-cry for More Kingdom Laborers! From here forward, I will seek to live as Christ's "hands and feet" wherever I go.

2. Everyday, ordinary people just like me are God's master plan for reaching the world. With God's guidance and power, I will live a life of love as an active Kingdom Laborer.

3. As God is calling me to be a channel of His love and truth, I will intentionally see, stop, and spend time with people in the mainstreams of life—up-close, one life at a time.

4. While I do not have what it takes on my own to get over myself and into God's plan, "I can do all things *through Christ* who strengthens me!" Therefore, I will daily seek to love Jesus more—enabling the greatest gift I give the world around me to be my own intimacy with God.

5. God has designed me with a unique ministry purpose in

mind. I will allow Him to employ my spiritual gifts, my passions, my talents, my personality, my strengths, my weaknesses, my experiences, my interests, my personal tragedies, my past failures, my assets, and anything and everything else about me to minister to others.

6. I acknowledge that God has shown up in my life and therefore I have stories to share! I will make it my priority to point others to Jesus and His Good News as I share my God-Stories.

7. I believe ministry to others does not just happen as a planned event on my terms and in my timing. I will listen for and obey the Holy Spirit's "along the way" leadings, taking the opportunity to engage others in the ordinary moments and places of my daily life.

8. While the needs of the world are far too overwhelming for one individual, I recognize the power of spiritual multiplication. Therefore, I will fuel Jesus' growing Laborership movement, intentionally investing in others—one life at a time.

I choose to be God's Kingdom Laborer
every day, everywhere!

Signature: _____

Date: _____

ANSWER KEY

JESUS' MISSION

Page 1
impact
mission

Page 2
laborers
laborers
More Kingdom Laborers
up-front leaders

Page 3
every person
ordinary
ordinary
done
most
Everything
intimacy
Neighbor
nearest

Page 4
Advance
mobile
More Kingdom Laborers

Page 6
Jesus

Page 7
close
impact
stream
everywhere

Page 8
one
just

Page 9
See
saw
seen
Stop
named
name

Page 10
Spend time with
T-I-M-E
You

JESUS' DEFINITION OF MINISTRY

Page 14
good
ministry
do something
need
love

Page 15
Unqualified

Page 16
unqualified
nobodies
Imperfect
point
Unworthy
worthy

Page 17
Sin-soiled
value
Unknowledgeable
with
Fearful

Page 18
Unloving
His
Unintentional
aimlessly
prayer

Page 21
not used
uniquely
masterpiece

Page 22
employ
spiritual gifts
hobbies
places
past experiences
tragedies, pain, suffering
uniform
camouflage

Page 23
enable, empower
obey

YOUR GOD-STORIES POINT TO JESUS

Page 29
shared
God-Stories

Page 30
bridge
showed up
change
simple
Christianese, church
anywhere, anytime, anyone
statements, pray

Page 35
question
ready

SPIRIT-DIRECTED LABORING

Page 45

final, first
fulfill

Page 46

Month	Speak to 365 per 4 months (+)	Equip 1 every 4 months (x)
4	**365**	**2**
8	**730**	**4**
12	**1,095**	**8**
16	**1,460**	**16**
20	**1,825**	**32**
24	**2,190**	**64**
28	**2,555**	**128**
32	**2,920**	**256**
36	**3,285**	**512**
40	**3,650**	**1,024**
...100	**9,125**	**16,736,256**
...136	**12,475**	**8.5 billion**

multiply
One
More, less, greater

Page 47

wealth
information
Empower
Our Role
never
multiplied

YOUR DECISION?

Page 53

all, all, all
love
one

MORE FROM FORGE

FORGE SPEAKERS & EVENTS
ForgeSpeakers.org

Need someone to challenge your group to become passionate followers of Jesus who live with hearts on fire and lives on purpose? Book a Forge speaker for your next event!

FORGE EQUIPPING PROGRAMS for ALL AGES
ForgeTraining.org

Forge Equipping is not summer camp and training events "as usual." Forge challenges and equips people of all ages to become unique, lifelong Kingdom laborers every day, everywhere.

FORGE BOOKS & RESOURCES
ForgeResources.org

Looking for a deeper relationship with God and practical ways to widen His Kingdom impact through your life? Forge has the resources you need.

THE FORGE APP
Essential Kingdom Laboring tools right at your fingertips:
TheForgeApp.org

JOIN THE MULTIPLYING MOVEMENT
Where everyday followers become Kingdom multipliers:
MultiplyingMovements.com

FORGE VIDEO CONTENT
Subscribe to free video content:
Youtube.com/ForgeForward

FORGE PODCAST
FuelForTheHarvest.com

FORGE DAILY TEXTS
Scan the QR code or visit ForgeForward.org/Sparks
to join Spark of the Day
for one-sentence daily devotionals.

NEED PRAYER?
Email us at Prayer@ForgeForward.org

CONTACT US
14485 E. Evans Avenue
Denver, Colorado 80014
303.745.8191
info@forgefoward.org

Learn more and get involved at
ForgeForward.org